I0510901

OPENING DAY

A BIG IDEA IN A LITTLE BOOK

EDWARD M. RILEY

ALSO BY THE AUTHOR:

My Monster and Me

To my editor, professor, mentor and friend

Linda G. Foss,

*without your love, guidance and support I would have
never been able to complete this, or many of the other
projects along the way. I am so grateful that you saw the
writer in me and was able to help
me see the writer in myself.*

....

*A special thanks to my friend Joli Winsett
of Winsett Creative. Her guidance and patience was
instrumental in making this project possible, and creating
my vision from dream into reality.*

FOREWORD

Edward M. Riley has written a charming story about the important and positive values that a father can teach his children. Set in the perhaps mundane world of a family-owned small town grocery store, the young man is a careful observer who seems to quickly learn that what people say is not nearly as meaningful as what they do. Often, the behaviors witnessed seemed quite contrary to the young man's concept of running a successful business as he thought every action should lead to some immediate benefit for the business.

Other behavior on the part of his father seemed almost obsessive but the young man learns how these actions and behaviors fit together as part of a value system, one that provided the customers far more than bread and milk.

"Opening Day" provides an important reminder that the consistent and sincere application of straightforward values can act to create a philosophy worth living by. That message will always be important in life and in business.

Larry S. McGee
Associate Dean, Baccalaureate Programs, retired
Centralia College

CHAPTER 1
WHY HIM?

"Restaurant of the Year"– for the second year in a row!

This was actually the fifth award of its kind in the ten years I'd been running my business.

Life was good. People asked—what made your business so special? What principles were behind your success?

They wanted to know how I could achieve such a feat – someone with no formal training – someone who didn't have a big budget to start – someone with very little experience—if someone like me could do it, then there must be some sort of secret.

I always answered by giving all of the credit to my dad and his influence in my life. True, but this wasn't all of it. It didn't really answer the question completely.

In this day and age, when businesses with high quality products and services seem to be few and far between, I was thinking about sharing my ideas. It wasn't as though I had been hoarding my principles. It just hadn't occurred to me that others would need to be told. Didn't most people conduct their lives and businesses in this manner? Over the years I'd become painfully aware that they don't.

Though this is a simple philosophy, a simple set of principles, to travel down this road is not easy. It takes patience, complete commitment, and setting the ego aside. However…the rewards are immeasurable.

A decade or so ago while considering going into business for myself, I was a bit frightened and perhaps confused. Growing up I had seen my father struggle to keep his own small business afloat during the recession. These difficulties resurfaced again when a brand new strip mall with a big box store was built just half a mile away, presenting a completely new set of challenges. And yet, his business prevailed. It didn't seem to matter how often he was presented with adversity or what challenges he faced, he always came out on top.

We lived in a small town in which the economy was based on the success of the paper mill. Often, the workers would go out on strike and the economy would take a nose dive, sending other small businesses in the community plummeting. My dad's business seemed somewhat immune to this economic disease.

I watched with curiosity as the small businesses around him came and went, yet he continued to survive. Not only survive, but my father's business thrived. And yet, his business wasn't special, state-of-the art, or trendy; it was just a local grocery store. I was perplexed. How could this be? If I was going to open my own business, I needed to know the beliefs and principles that drove his success.

With that said, here is my story.

CHAPTER II

ALICE

One of the things I remember most vividly about my dad's business was the familiarity with the people he worked with. Over time, I came to know these people as family. They were my adoptive aunts and uncles. I grew up with their children. We celebrated holidays and special occasions with them in our home. Birthdays, anniversaries and weddings were never missed.

Alice was one of the checkers at my dad's store. When her husband died suddenly of a heart attack, he and my mother dropped everything to be with her.

I found out years later that Alice's husband didn't have insurance at the time of his death. She had no family to turn to, but that's when my parents, the staff, and customers rallied around her in support, helping to make arrangements and cover the cost of the funeral.

At the time, Alice had been working for my father for less than a month! Several years later she fell in love and married Dave, an accountant at the store. Dad actually took time off so that he and my mother could help with the preparations. As he walked her down the aisle he seemed as proud of Alice as if she were his own daughter.

How could taking time off to help someone be good for business? And yet, he never seemed to hesitate when doing this sort of thing. He believed that just like his family, his employees were not there to serve him. Instead, he was there to serve them. He was often asked how he had achieved such incredible staff loyalty. It was simple: his staff weren't a commodity to be used up, they were an asset to be nurtured and grown.

Over the years, he always provided for their needs. He treated his staff with the utmost respect and dignity. They gave of themselves freely without hesitation. The fear of being used by management, often commonplace in other businesses, did not exist. This humane treatment had a profound effect on people. It went a long, long way.

When dad had a goal for the store, he would share it with everyone. He would tell them what he wanted to accomplish, ask for their input, and then hand the project over to them to implement. He trusted them. They, in turn, felt a sense of ownership so his goals became their goals. He knew that without a strong staff and their constant support, he would not have been able to reach any of his goals. He knew this, and never hesitated in letting them know how important they were.

It's interesting to note, how their loyalty affected me growing up. At the store Dad would call me over and introduce me as his 'pride and joy.' Staff members would always make a big fuss. He'd give me a kiss on the forehead and scruff up my hair. I always protested with an 'Aw Dad,' sincerely hoping this ritual would come to an end. It didn't.

Later during visits home, catching up with staff, or our extended family as they really were, I had to endure this silly ritual. My father still treated me as his little boy, his 'pride and joy.' Growing older I minded it less and less. As a man I finally understood.

CHAPTER III
WHAT MEANS THE MOST

Over the years I watched my dad interact with his customers. When a new customer came into the store, he would introduce himself, shaking hands vigorously. Then he'd take them by the arm and introduce them to the rest of the staff as if they were old friends. He would even include other customers in the introduction, talking about families, who was having babies, birthdays, and so on.

He often sent cards: birthday, congratulations, condolence, whatever the occasion called for. If he knew about it, he responded. He always let his customers know how much he personally cared for them, each and every one of them. I watched with aw as he always proved how much he cared by his actions. This wasn't some kind of act.

When the local river flooded, causing quite a bit of damage to several sections of town, it left some families without food or shelter. To add insult to injury, they didn't have flood insurance –none of us did back then. According to the insurance companies, the whole town was in a flood plain and was considered high risk, which meant that insurance wasn't available.

When my father heard about their plight, he sprang into action. First, he set up store accounts for all of the affected families so that they could at least get the basics like food and toiletries. Next, he started a drive by putting donation jars at every checkout stand so that other people could contribute. The jars became so popular that eventually every shop in town had one. He and Mom would spend hours after work, driving around town collecting money, and organizing it for deposit into a trust account that had been set up for these families.

One thing led to another. Dad ultimately spearheaded a local grassroots movement to advocate for those who lived in flood plains. Eventually the pressure across the country led the government to take on the insurance industry to mandate national flood coverage.

My dad always seemed willing to get involved with the community. Whenever the mill would go out on strike, which was about every four years when their contracts were up for negotiation, my father was known for extending credit to his customers. Mind you, this meant that they gave him only their 'word' for collateral, nothing more.

Of course, this commitment to community could have drawbacks for a young boy. Because Dad was always looking to help someone in the community, I often became part of the equation and was volunteered for some neighborly task that was usually unpleasant in one way or another.

My personal reflection aside, Dad's faith in his customers has paid him back in customer loyalty. Not a single person ever backed out of their commitment to my father. Why? Because he treated each and every customer with respect and generosity. They, in turn, were so loyal to him that they would drive miles out of their way to shop at his store.

I recall the day when a customer was once again commenting on the long drive he made. He asked, "Why are your prices always lower than other places? How can you afford to operate this way?"

"What's fair to some manufacturers isn't what I think is fair. They don't live here, you and I do. Marking things up above their true value is price gouging in my opinion. It'll be a cold day in hell before that's allowed in my store," my dad replied.

Then there was what Dad called survival items, so basic household items were barely marked up at all. He wasn't going to be the person to make a profit on someone's survival. For my dad it was more important that his customers could afford to shop at his store, than for him to make more profit. I think this was another way of his giving back to his customers in return for their loyalty and support.

CHAPTER IV
A GOOD MAN

Speaking of giving back to his customers... there was a young woman who lived down the street from the store. At the time I was in my teens and she was probably not much older when her husband abandoned her and their two small children.

Whenever she came into the store, Dad would slip things into her cart when she wasn't looking. He accompanied her around the store teasing the kids along the way. By the time they got to the check stand, the cart would be brimming over. They just kept talking about the weather, or something, as he would casually ring up the items. "I really need to train the staff to mark things more clearly," he'd say. This or that was always on special. He couldn't possibly charge full price for dented cans.

By the time he was finished, the final bill amounted to half of what it should have been. This wasn't the end of it. He would then call me over to load her cart and push it the four blocks to her house, and help unload it.

The only time I ever saw her acknowledge this ritual was one day at the store. She walked up to my father, whispered something in his ear, and then gave him a big hug. His eyes welled up while tears were streaming down her face. I was curious of course, but just kept loading the cart.

During the walk to her house, she never said a word. I unloaded the groceries, as usual. As I started to walk away, she took my hand, looked me straight in the eye, and simply said, "You are a very lucky young man. Your father is a good man, always remember that." She moved away soon after.

When I asked Dad why he gave so freely to people, he explained it this way: "Son, if you aren't busy helping others, then you're probably too busy worrying about your own problems."

CHAPTER V
ONLY THE BEST

Another thing about my dad's store was his constant eye for detail. He was always cleaning something or rearranging merchandise to be more convenient for customers. Once a week he put up new banners or streamers so that the place always looked fresh and new. Everything in the place was spotless – always – from the parking lot to the coolers. He didn't miss a thing.

As a teenager I had decided to test him. I put a small piece of wadded up paper in an obscure corner of the store to see how long it would take him to notice. Minutes – it was only a matter of minutes! Unbelievable, nothing got by him.

Dad had the highest of standards. For instance, if a delivery arrived that didn't meet his expectations, he wouldn't hesitate in returning it. If a delivery man complained about the extra hassle, he would say nothing and point to the huge sign that hung over the entrance:

"It's a funny thing about life;
If you refuse to accept anything but the best,
You very often get it."
Somerset Maugham

He held the same high standards for his staff. He was always working on ways to offer them better benefits or higher wages. If someone got hurt or became ill, he never hesitated in sending them home or to the doctor, with pay of course.

I remember when one of the stock boys, Brad, fell badly, hurting his back. My father was so concerned that he personally drove him to the doctors' office, then home helping him to bed. The next morning, dad left early in order to check on Brad. My mom was in on it too, having cooked and prepared individual meals for him the night before. Dad not only dropped these off but took the time to ensure Brad was comfortable before heading to the store. I discovered years later that my dad had paid for a massage therapist to help Brad with his physical therapy and recovery. Of course, this extra help enabled the young man to return to work more rapidly.

Brad went on to become the assistant manager at my dad's store, and later opened his own store in another town. He and Dad continued to talk on the phone regularly for years. I heard that his store even looks similar to my dad's. Clearly he learned from my dad's example.

Dad lived his life striving for perfection. Most of the time, he reached his goals, but not always. But that didn't seem to matter to him. He felt that the pursuit of perfection, not the achievement, was the important part. As long as you were striving for the best in your life, in business, and in your personal matters, then you were on the right track. If you failed sometimes that was O.K., as long as you brushed yourself off and tried again.

CHAPTER VI

THE DRIVING FORCE

It was time to find out what drove my dad's success, at work and in life. Since I was getting ready to open my own business, I wanted to know how he always seemed to succeed.

Was it loyal employees, committed customers, fair pricing, quality products, his eye for detail? What did giving back to the community have to do with it? And by the way, how could he and his staff really be so happy at work?

So, I took him out to lunch. I told him I had something important to talk to him about. I was, of course completely prepared. I had my newly organized business plan, my financial figures and feasibility study. I also had made a report on my observations about the success of his store.

He sat there listening intently. When I was all done he sat up in his chair and said "Son, it's about one single principle. I call it Opening Day." Then he sat back in his chair with a big grin on his face.

"Opening Day!? How could an entire business philosophy be hinged on that one phrase? It just didn't make sense."

He stopped me right there. "Son, think about it for a moment. Opening Day isn't just one day, it's every day!"

Well, this just confused me even more. How could you have Opening Day, every day? All of that work, all of that preparation, all of that excitement?

He went on to explain that it was a very simple concept and that I didn't need to make it so complex. "Simple," he said, "If you have Opening Day, every day, then that means you treat your customers like they're important, yes? And if it's Opening Day every day, then that means you're going to treat your employees the same way, like they're important, yes?"

Hmm… why not make every single day 'Opening Day?' Why not make an Opening Day impression every single day!! I was starting to get it.

That, of course, explained why his business always looked so good and why he had such an eye for detail. But what about his employees? He certainly could have paid them a little less, like everyone else. And what about helping his customers? He didn't have to give them credit, or loan them money, or charge so little. Why did he do all of that?

Leaning forward Dad asked, "You still don't get it, do you? You see, every day is Opening Day. That means I have the opportunity every moment of every day to make the best impression I can. But it's not just about business, it's also about life."

He went on to explain, "In my life, there is no tomorrow. There is no yesterday. There is only today. There is only right now! That means simply, that I'm given the opportunity to offer the best of myself every moment. And I do. If I fail to offer the best that I can, then I have cheated myself and others."

"So, you live your life as if every day is Opening Day? How could lower prices and helping that lady and her kids and…"

"Here let me help you," dad interrupted. "What do I do for a living?"

"You sell groceries," I said.

"Not quite," he said.

"My business has very little to do with selling groceries. You see, son, I'm in the business of helping people; selling groceries is only part of what I do."

Okay, now I really was confused.

He went on to explain that what every business really does, or should do, is help people. Selling stuff is only one aspect of doing that. If people were only concentrating on that, then they aren't living up to their full potential.

"Obviously, this carries into your personal life as well. You only have one shot, son.

That's today! So, take it!"

That's when it all made sense. From that moment on, I knew exactly what he meant. We really do only have the here and now. That means today, moment by moment. Why waste the opportunity to make a difference?

CHAPTER VII

LIVING AN 'OPENING DAY' LIFE

Back then I knew that I wanted to make an impact. I wanted to make a difference in people's lives, instead of just trudging through my life complaining. I am proud to say that since that day, over ten years ago, I've tried to make every day my 'Opening Day.'

It's so simple and here are the principles I try to live by.

I CREATE A LOYAL STAFF...

Staff loyalty is one of the most important aspects of the 'Opening Day.' I learned from my dad that without it, all of the other pieces fall flat. Here are the guidelines I use in developing these relationships.

- I praise my staff for a job well done. Whatever I do, I don't mix the praise with a reprimand or correction. It negates the praise. I build people up; I don't tear them down.
- I respect my staff and their feelings. They are people, after all. Asking people to do something with

a simple please and thank you goes a long way. A lot farther than any demand.

- I treat my employees with dignity. They are vital to this equation. Remember, it doesn't really matter if I'm the boss or not.
- I delegate projects and tasks for the staff to implement, then simply walk away. I believe in them. More often than not, they know the best way to give the customers what they want and need.
- I trust my staff and have faith that they will do the right thing. They might not always succeed, but if I give them the right tools, I'm never surprised at how far they will go.

I CREATE DEDICATED CUSTOMERS...

Today's customers are very savvy. If I don't treat them right, there is a business right around the corner that will. So often we see businesses putting all of their effort into gimmicks and specials.

- I offer fair prices every day, not gimmicks to create dedicated long-term customers. It's not really a special or sale if it happens every week.
- I am always honest. This goes a long way with customers. They trust me, and wouldn't consider going elsewhere.
- I'm involved in my community. This is vital in business, especially in today's environment. I don't blow my own horn about this because it would look like a gimmick and my sincerity would be in question.

- I keep my word no matter what. Of course sometimes mistakes are made or there are situations that are out of my control. When this happens I make every effort to be upfront and honest, trying to make it right. This earns my customers' faith.

I GIVE OF MYSELF...

Being a giving person is the greatest gift you can give…. to yourself.

- I give to my community. Many businesses give to their communities, but do so loudly and only as a marketing tool. I give without hidden motivation, because I care about my community.
- I treat everyone with respect and dignity. I achieve this simply by being subtle and discreet. Small gestures can make a big difference in someone's life when they are in need.
- I give without expectation. After all, that's not what it's all about. Giving isn't about bartering or what I can get in return. The true gift is in the giving itself, and that being enough.

I OFFER ONLY THE BEST...

Offering only the best applies to many things in life, not just products and services. If I'm not offering the best that I have to offer, then people aren't seeing the real me… the best me!

- I offer the highest quality products available. This means that I don't skimp when I choose what I offer, even when it costs a bit more to do so.
- I keep my business clean and well maintained. I don't wait until things look rundown to make improvements; my customers really appreciate that things always look fresh and new.
- I offer the best wage and benefits package available to my employees. This allows them to be their best at home, work, and in our community.
- I realize offering the best isn't perfection, and never will be. I wouldn't have it any other way. First, there is no such thing as perfection in my mind, and if there was, then I wouldn't have any room for improvement. I'd rather keep working for that improvement.

CHAPTER VIII
MY HERO

My father died just over two years ago. The day we had the funeral was one of the saddest days of my life. It was also one of the proudest days of my life. The city actually had to close down the street where my dad's store is located because of the turnout. It seems my father had more of an impact on our community than anyone could have imagined. People flew in from all over the country to pay their respects.

Many came up to me, shook my hand, gave me hugs and told me stories as to what an impact he had made on their lives. The one that meant the most was a woman who came up, kids in tow, and introduced herself as Maria. Then she introduced her husband and each one of her children. When she got to the youngest, a lanky blond boy, she paused for a moment, smiling softly. She tousled his hair fondly and then introduced him as Tommy.

"My dad's name was Tom," I said. "I know," she replied with a big smile. "I actually named him after your father. You see, when you were a boy I was the woman you used to help home with my groceries. The woman who was so sad all of the time. After my first husband left me and my children, I was so afraid and alone. I had no family and no one to help, except your dad. Without his generosity and kindness I don't think I could have made it. His compassion gave me the confidence I needed to go on; for that I will always be grateful."

"After I remarried, I had another baby and chose to name him after your father. I thought you might like to know." Maria then gave the boy a big squeeze, him protesting with an "Aw Mom." She started to walk away but stopped and turned, "You are a very lucky boy; your father is a good man. Always remember that."

It was at that moment that I realized what a huge impact Dad had on people's lives; he had truly lived an 'Opening Day' life. That meant he touched people on a genuine and heartfelt level. It also meant that he had a rich and fulfilling life.

More than that, I realized that he had given me the best gift a man could give his son.

He gave me the principles to live my life everyday as 'Opening Day.'

ABOUT THE AUTHOR

 With a background in education writing and a medical massage career spanning 20 years, Edward M. Riley has developed a wide range of interests. From whimsical children's books, to motivational books that inspire, he has become a prolific writer, often weaving life lessons and morals learned from his own life into his work. Bringing a sense of reality to each one of his stories, he creates real-life characters that any reader can identify with. In addition, Edward continues to write instructional books on advanced techniques for those in the massage industry.